PROPERTY OF
SUSQUENITA SCHOOLS NO. _____

STUDENT	YEAR

PROPERTY OF
SUSQUENITA SCHOOLS NO. _____

STUDENT	YEAR

SIMPLE MACHINES AND HOW THEY WORK

ELIZABETH N. SHARP

Simple machines and how they work

Illustrated by Ida Scheib

THIS EDITION IS PRINTED AND DISTRIBUTED BY SPECIAL
ARRANGEMENT WITH THE ORIGINATORS AND PUBLISHERS,
Random House, Inc., NEW YORK, BY

E. M. HALE AND COMPANY
EAU CLAIRE, WISCONSIN

Contents

SIMPLE MACHINES AND HOW THEY WORK

1

Machines help us

Long ago people had few machines. Most things were made with simple tools. Of course, this took much longer than with machines.

For example, roads were once built with garden tools. The workmen used shovels to dig dirt and move it. A man can carry only a few pounds of dirt in a shovel.

Today we have huge machines to move earth. One of these machines can carry more earth than a thousand shovels.

We need big machines to build big highways. A big machine can cut a roadway through a hill. It can carry the dirt to fill up a swamp.

There are machines to do almost anything you can think of Machines can wash clothes or plant seeds or milk cows. They can drive nails or paint houses. The dentist has a machine that cleans your teeth.

The automobile is a machine. So is the airplane. It used to be called the flying machine.

Every machine makes work easier and faster.

You could sharpen your pencil with a knife. But a pencil sharpener is easier and faster.

Some machines are big and complicated. Others are very simple. Every big machine is made of many simple little machines that work together.

For example, an automobile has dozens of wheels that work in different ways. Each wheel is a simple machine.

A screw is another simple machine. Wedges and pulleys are simple machines, too.

Without these simple machines, the big machines could not work. If you understand the simple machines, you can understand the complicated ones.

2

Simple wheels

The first people on earth had no wheels. They had
no wagons and no wheelbarrows. They had to carry
or drag everything they wanted to move.

Probably the earliest WHEEL was a rolling log.
People saw that something round moves easily
because it rolls over and over. So when the early
men wanted to move heavy stones, they put logs

6

The first wheel was probably a rolling log.

under them. Then they pushed against the stones. The logs rolled forward, and the stones moved with them.

This was much easier than dragging the stones along the ground. And it meant that much bigger stones could be moved.

Here is an experiment in two parts. It will show you why the early men were glad to move stones with logs:

(1) Put a piece of string through a thin rubber band. Tie the string around a heavy book. Put the book on the table. Then put one finger into the rubber band.

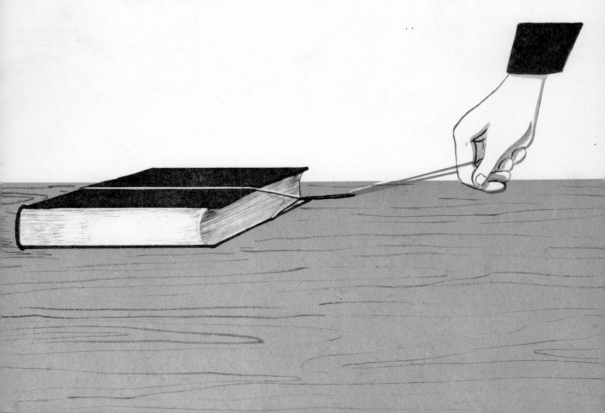

Now, pull the book along the table. The rubber band stretches. The book is hard to pull because it rubs or drags.

This rubbing or dragging is called FRICTION. Friction makes anything hard to move. If we cut down friction, work is easier.

(2) Now put three round pencils under the book.

Pull the book again with one finger in the rubber band. The rubber band doesn't stretch as much as before. The book is easier to pull. This is because the pencils act as rollers. They work like the logs used by early men. They cut down friction.

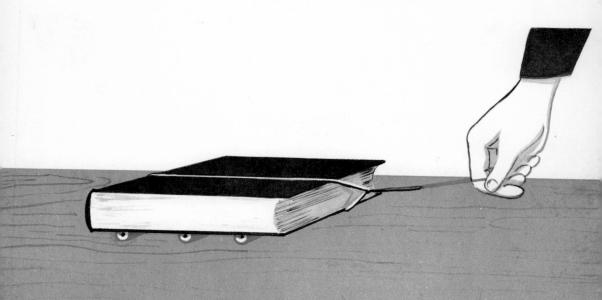

You can make a model of a wheel and axle.

You can make a model of a simple wheel. Cut a circle out of cardboard. Then push a pencil halfway through the center of the circle.

The pencil is the AXLE. Hold the pencil firmly. Try to spin the cardboard wheel. It won't spin fast. That is because the cardboard rubs against the pencil. Your wheel is being slowed down by friction.

Sometimes we want wheels to go slowly. When someone learns to roller-skate, he uses beginner's skates. These skates have wheels that rub against the axle. The skater cannot go very fast. Friction helps him while he is learning.

3

Wheels with ball
bearings

In most machines we want the wheels to go fast.
We try to cut down the friction.

A good skater wants to go fast. His skates have
wheels that spin with very little friction. That is
because these skates have BALL BEARINGS.

Each wheel has small steel balls between the axle

12

and the wheel. As the wheel turns, it touches these balls. They roll against the axle.

Hold a skate upside down and spin one wheel. Do you hear a clicking sound? If you do, the skate has ball bearings. As the wheels turn, the little steel balls hit each other. They make the clicking sound.

The wheel of a ball bearing skate turns faster and spins longer than a simple wheel. With ball

Between the wheel and the axle are the ball bearings.

13

bearings, a wheel *rolls around* the axle. Without ball bearings, it *rubs against* the axle. The ball bearings cut down friction.

You can make a model of ball bearings. You will need some marbles of the same size. You will also need three jar lids of different sizes.

Put the smallest lid inside the middle-size lid. Put a ring of marbles around the edge of the small lid. (*Step No. 1 in the picture.*)

Next, cover these two lids with the largest lid. Be sure that it rests on the marbles and does not touch the table. (*Step No. 2.*)

Now put a book on the top lid and spin it. (*Step No. 3.*) The book will turn easily. That is because the marbles turn as the lid turns.

The marbles act like the steel ball bearings in a wheel. They are the *balls* that *bear* the weight of the turning wheel. They cut down the friction between the axle and the wheel.

Now take out the marbles. Put the top lid back and put the book on it. Try to spin the book. It won't spin. It will only move slowly. There is too much friction without the ball bearings.

14

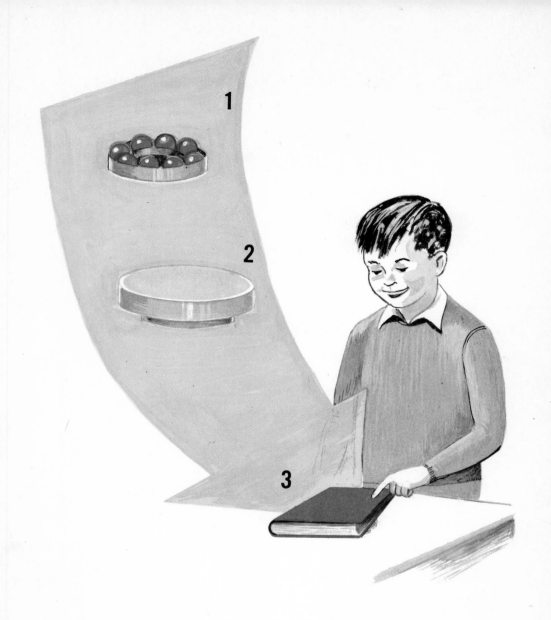

1

2

3

You can make a model of ball bearings.

15

Wheels that move fast have ball bearings around their axles. You can't see them. But ball bearings are in the wheels of bicycles, automobiles, locomotives, and airplanes. They are in electric fans and food mixers. They are in hundreds of other machines.

Ball bearings are made in many sizes. Some are smaller than the head of a pin. These are used in very small machines. Some are the size of marbles. And some are as big as oranges.

4

Wheels that turn
other wheels

Often a job is made easier if one wheel turns another wheel. A good example is the egg beater— the kind you turn by hand.

Notice the teeth in the big wheel of an egg beater. These teeth join with the teeth in the two little wheels.

The handle turns the big wheel. The teeth of the

An egg beater makes work easier.

big wheel make the little wheels go around. And the little wheels turn the blades that beat the eggs.

The interesting thing is that the blades go much faster than the handle you turn. You can see for yourself. Put a crayon mark on one blade of an egg beater. Now turn the handle slowly, one time around. Count how many times the crayon mark goes around. You will probably see it four or five times.

This means you can beat eggs much faster with an egg beater than with a fork. The egg beater makes work easier because it has a wheel that turns other wheels.

A doorknob is also a machine with a big wheel that turns a little wheel.

A doorknob is a simple machine.

19

In a bicycle, one wheel turns another.

20

The big, round part in your hand is like a big wheel. The axle goes all the way through the door and connects inside with the door latch. But this axle is really a little wheel. It turns either way.

Because the knob is big, you can open the door easily. If you took off the knob, you couldn't turn the little axle easily with your fingers.

Sometimes one wheel turns another with a chain. You have seen this in a bicycle.

The wheel connected to the pedals has teeth. The small wheel connected to the big back wheel also has teeth. The chain fits into the teeth of both wheels.

Turn the bike upside down. Use your hand to push a pedal around once. Watch the two wheels with teeth. As the larger one turns, the little one turns, too. But the little one goes faster. It goes faster because it is smaller.

The big back wheel of the bike also goes faster. It is connected to the little wheel that has teeth. Every time the little wheel turns around, the back wheel turns with it.

You can go faster and farther with a bike than on your own feet. Make this test:

Lay a stick on the ground as a marker. Put the bike right side up with the back wheel against the stick. Get one pedal as high as it will go. Put your foot on this pedal.

Now hop aboard. Push that pedal down and up to the top again. Stop as soon as it gets to the top.

You have really taken two steps. One step was down with one leg. The other step was down with your other leg. Mark how far the back wheel of your bike moved from the stick.

Now see how many steps you must take to cover the same distance on foot. Is it four steps? Or five steps? Or even more?

22

With a bicycle, you can travel faster than on foot.

23

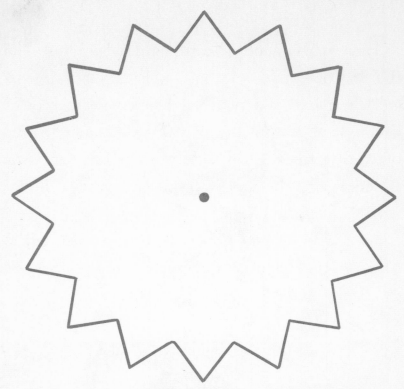

For an experiment, make two wheels this size.

You can make a model of wheels that touch, as in the egg beater. Trace the wheel on this page. Paste the tracing on stiff cardboard. The backing from a pad of writing paper is a good kind of cardboard to use.

Now cut out your first cardboard wheel. Cut the teeth very carefully, so that they are exactly the same size.

Then make another cardboard wheel just like the first one.

Take a nail and punch a hole in the center of each wheel. Fasten the two wheels to a big piece of cardboard, side by side. Use paper fasteners. Be sure that the teeth of the two wheels fit together, as in the picture on this page.

Turn one wheel. Notice that the other wheel turns in the opposite direction. But both wheels go at the same speed.

The wheels turn in opposite directions.

For another experiment, make one wheel this size.

Now trace the wheel on this page. Paste the tracing on cardboard and cut it out carefully.

Fasten the small wheel to the cardboard, next to one of the big wheels. Be sure the teeth fit together.

Turn the big wheel. The small one will go faster.

These wheels must be made very carefully. But they will be fun to experiment with.

5

A crank that acts
like a wheel

Sometimes a handle or crank acts like a big wheel to turn a smaller wheel. Take a look at a pencil sharpener.

Watch the end of the handle as you turn it. It makes a circle in the air. The circle is like a wheel.

The handle turns two little wheels inside the

The handle of a pencil sharpener works like a wheel.

28

case. These little wheels are at the ends of rollers. The rollers have sharp blades that shave the wood from your pencil.

The sharpener is faster and smoother than a knife. And it won't cut your finger.

Another kind of crank is on a meat grinder. The handle is much longer than on a pencil sharpener. A longer crank means more power. You might think that some meat is harder to grind than wood. It is.

The first automobiles were started by a crank. The crank was at the bottom of the radiator, between the front wheels. Often the crank was very hard to turn.

Many women were not strong enough to start a car. Drivers often got mad when their engine stopped in traffic. They had to get out of the car to crank the engine.

These troubles ended when the electric starter was invented. Electricity now does the work that used to be done by hand and arm. The driver steps on a button or turns a switch to start the engine. Only a very few old cars still have cranks.

6

Wheels with ropes

The PULLEY is a special kind of wheel. It does work that no other wheel can do.

It has no smooth rim for rolling along the ground. It has no teeth for turning another wheel.

Instead it has a groove all around its edge. A rope fits into this groove.

There is a pulley at the top of every flagpole. A rope loops over the pulley and comes down on each side to the ground.

The person who raises the flag ties it to the rope on one side. Then he pulls down on the other side of the rope. Up goes the flag.

The pulley changes the direction of pull. You pull down on one rope to make the other rope go up.

Without pulleys, it would be very hard to raise a flag. Somebody would have to shinny up the flagpole every morning. He would have to go up again at sundown to bring the flag down. Of

course, this would be quite interesting to watch—especially in rainy weather.

A pulley seems to have two ropes. Sometimes it has only one rope that makes a long loop around the pulley. You can pull and pull, but you will never get to the end. It's like a very long rubber band.

Pulleys are used for clothes lines in big cities.

One pulley is fastened to the house, next to a window. The other pulley is on a post or wall some distance away. The loop of rope makes two lines between the pulleys.

The woman who hangs out the wash stands at her window. She pins some socks on the lower rope and pushes it away. She pins on some shirts and

34

pushes the rope farther away. She pins on towels and pajamas and keeps pushing.

When the laundry is dry, she pulls it in. First the pajamas and towels come off the rope. Then the shirts. Then the socks.

All this is possible because the pulleys change the direction of pull.

Pulleys are used in hundreds of different ways.

On a sailboat there is a pulley at the top of the mast. The sailor pulls down on the rope to raise the sail.

Farmers use pulleys to lift big bundles of hay. Pulleys help to lift the hay from wagons to the upper floor of a barn.

Building workers use pulleys to lift steel beams from the street to higher floors.

Sometimes several pulleys work together.

Painters stand on a scaffold to paint the sides of a building. They have no engines to pull their scaffold to the top. They have only their arms.

This scaffold is heavy. The painters weigh a lot, too. And they must carry buckets of paint, brushes, and tools.

How can the painters pull this heavy load from the ground to the top of the building?

The answer is that they use pulleys with two wheels. These double pulleys are fastened to big iron hooks at the roof. And there are double pulleys fastened to the scaffold. Long ropes connect the pulleys at the roof with the pulleys at the scaffold.

With double pulleys, heavy loads can be raised slowly but very easily. The painters pull down several feet of rope to go up just one foot.

You might think the word *pulley* comes from the word *pull*. They certainly sound alike. But they are quite different words. Pulley comes from an old Greek word meaning *axle*.

You can experiment with small pulleys and cord. Small pulleys are sold in toy stores and in hardware stores. Try using them in different ways.

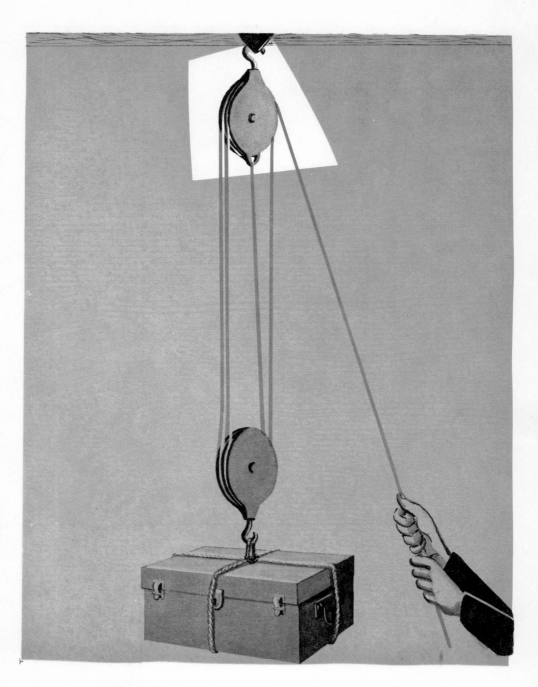

A double pulley helps lift something very heavy.

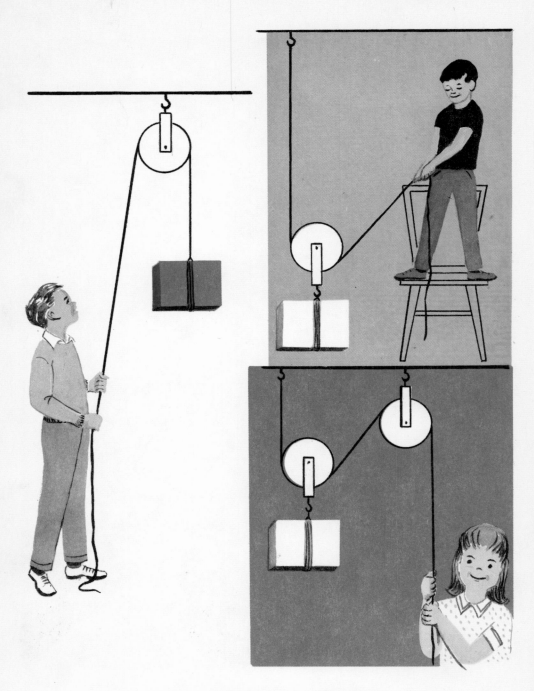

You can experiment with pulleys.

7

A slant that helps

The man in the picture on the next page has a problem. He wants to get the barrel up to the platform. The barrel is full of sugar. It is too heavy for him to lift.

There are no ropes or pulleys to lift the barrel. But there is a strong board near by. So the workman puts one end of the board against the plat-

form. The board is now slanting. Then he rolls
the barrel up the board. The barrel rolls like a
wheel.

The slanted board is a simple machine. It makes
work easier.

It is called an INCLINED PLANE.

A slanted board makes work easier.

A slanted board is an inclined plane.

A plane is a smooth, flat surface. A blackboard is a plane. So is a sidewalk. So is the side of a book.

If you lean one book against another, you will have an inclined plane. But don't try to roll a barrel of sugar up it!

There are many kinds of inclined planes. All of them make work easier.

A flight of steps is an inclined plane. Notice how the steps are slanted.

The steps are slanted because the slant makes them easier to climb. When steps are very steep, they are hard to climb. In the picture, there are three kinds of steps.

Which would be easiest to climb? The steps at the top of the picture, because they have the most slant.

Which would be next easiest? The stepladder in the middle, because it has some slant.

Which would be hardest to climb? The ladder on the side of the tank, because it goes straight up. It has no slant.

You can see how a slant makes work easier by trying an experiment. Pile up about a dozen books on the floor. Take a roller skate. Loop a thin rubber band around the front axle.

Now put one finger through the rubber band and lift the skate to the top of the books.

44

Steeper steps are harder to climb.

The rubber band will stretch a long way. You might think it would break. Maybe it will!

Next find a short board. Lean it against the books. Put the skate on the board. Put your finger in the rubber band and pull the skate to the top.

This time the rubber band doesn't stretch so much. You don't have to pull so hard. The skate goes up easily because the board is slanted.

And the wheels help, too. They carry much of the weight.

Now make an inclined plane by putting a much longer board against the pile of books.

You can pull the skate with the rubber band more easily than ever. The slant is not so steep. Most of the weight is on the wheels. You lift very little.

There are many kinds of inclined planes. Look at the driveways along a street. They slant from the road to the sidewalk. Each one is an inclined plane.

Often the roof of a house is an inclined plane. It has a slant so that the rain will run off. The drainboard of your kitchen sink is an inclined plane. It slopes, too, so that water will drain off.

A playground slide is an inclined plane. It is steep so that you can slide down fast.

Any sidewalk that slopes is an inclined plane. Any road that goes up or down a hill is an inclined plane. So is the hill itself.

Hills and mountains are the biggest inclined planes you can see anywhere.

What can you do when you come to a very steep hill? You can walk straight up. But that is the hard way. It is better to do what the animals do. Look at the paths made on steep hillsides by rabbits, woodchucks, deer, goats, horses, cows, and other animals.

These smart animals don't walk straight up. They make paths that have an easy slant. They zigzag.

This means they have to walk farther to reach the top. But their climb is much easier than a straight one.

When men build a road through the mountains, they do as the animals do. The road does not go straight up a steep slope. No automobile could climb it. So the highway has an easy slant.

8

Spirals and screws

The Statue of Liberty is one of the most famous statues in the world.

People go up inside the statue all the way to the crown. Then they look out the windows in the front of the crown.

Inside the statue, there are two sets of steps
all the way to the top. They wind around and
around.

These steps are a special kind of inclined plane,
called a SPIRAL.

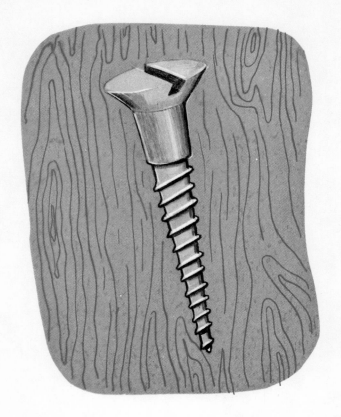

Another very common kind of spiral is the wood SCREW.

Screws hold things together. They are not smooth like nails. Their spiral is a little ridge that keeps twisting all the way to the point. When the screw is twisted into place, this ridge makes a tiny groove in the wood.

You can't pull out the screw with a hammer the

way you pull out a nail. You must twist the screw with a screw driver.

Screws hold much better than nails do. That is why screws are used for the hinges of heavy doors. They hold the hinges tight.

A screw is really an inclined plane. Let's see why. Draw this shape on a piece of paper:

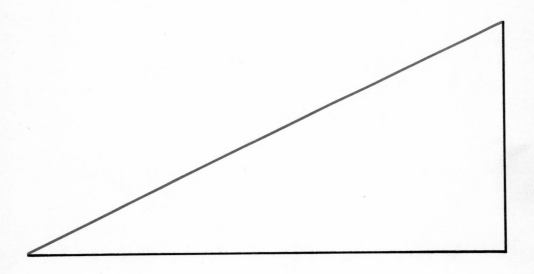

Make it about 6 inches long and 3 inches high. Make the long slanted line a different color. You have an inclined plane.

Now cut the shape out. Wrap your inclined plane around a pencil:

Wrap it all the way and hold it. Your colored line makes a spiral. The spiral is like the ridge of a screw. So a screw is really an inclined plane that spirals around a nail.

A screw can lift you.

A screw is a simple machine, too. Some kinds of screws are used for lifting. Perhaps you have lifted yourself with the screw of a piano stool.

If you turn the seat one way, it goes up. Turn it the other way and it goes down.

A big screw can lift a house.

Have you ever seen a house being raised so that it can be moved? A house is a very heavy thing to lift. But with strong screws, a few men can easily raise a house. The tool they use is called a jack screw.

Screws are good machines. They make hard work easy.

9

Wedges

The WEDGE was a good friend of the first settlers in America.

It is a simple little machine that can do a powerful job. Early settlers used a wedge to split wood. With a heavy hammer, the wedge was driven into a log.

An early American split wood with a wedge.

59

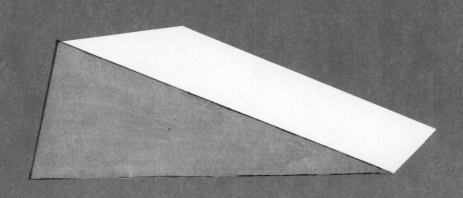

Take a closer look at the wedge.
The wedge slants like an inclined plane.

An ax blade is a wedge. It also splits wood.
Any tool that cuts is probably a wedge. The sharp
edge of a knife is a wedge. The blades of scissors
are wedges.
The point of a nail is a wedge.
A nail has a wedge point so that it can pry the

wood apart. If you try to hammer the wrong end of a nail into wood, you will see why you need a wedge. You may need a bandage, too.

Even needles and pins have wedges for points. A needle makes a tiny hole by prying apart the threads of cloth.

An ax blade is a wedge.

61

A woodpecker's bill is a sharp wedge.

There are many kinds of wedges in nature. You can find wedges in your own mouth. Just feel your front teeth between your thumb and finger.

Many animals have teeth that are wedges. The long, sharp teeth of dogs and cats are wedges. These wedges can tear meat apart.

Sharks and most other fishes have wedges for teeth.

How does a woodpecker drill a hole in the bark of a tree? He uses his bill, which is a sharp wedge.

Claws are wedges, too. They are very useful to birds and other animals. Hawks and owls use their claws to catch mice, fish, and small birds. Dogs use their claws to bury bones.

A dog's claws are wedges.

63

A crowbar makes work easier.

10

Simple levers

The man in the picture is lifting a big rock with a heavy iron bar called a crowbar. He couldn't move this rock with his hands alone. It is much too heavy.

When he pushes down on one end of the crowbar, the other end goes up. And the rock goes up, too.

The crowbar is another kind of machine. It is a LEVER. It does work a man cannot do by himself.

To see how a simple lever works, lay a yardstick on a block of wood. (*Step No. 1 in the picture.*)

Put a piece of brick or a small rock on the short end of the yardstick. Of course it will go down to the table. (*Step No. 2.*)

Now put a smaller piece of brick or rock on the long end. The small stone will go down and the big one will go up. (*Step No. 3.*)

Why does the small stone lift the big one? Because it is farther from the block of wood. This block is called the FULCRUM. Every lever has a fulcrum. It is the part that does not move.

The longer the lever is, the more you can lift. You can experiment by moving the yardstick back and forth on the fulcrum. If you get nearly all of the yardstick on one side of the fulcrum, it will lift a stone by itself. (*Step No. 4.*)

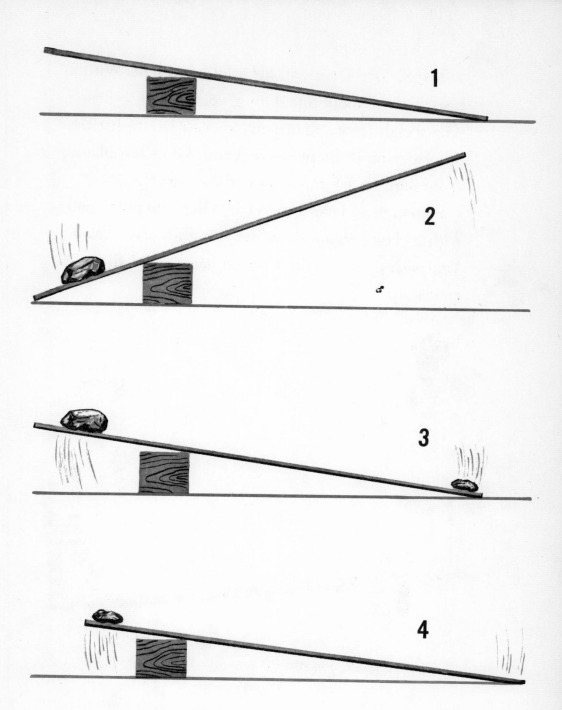

You can experiment with a lever.

A very long lever will lift a lot of weight. With a heavy board about 8 feet long, you can lift someone who weighs more than you do. You would lift the other person by stepping on your end of the plank.

Be sure to let the person down gently.

Sometimes a lever is curved. When you pull a nail with a claw hammer, you are using a curved lever. You push down on the wooden handle and the nail comes up.

With a lever, you can lift someone much heavier.

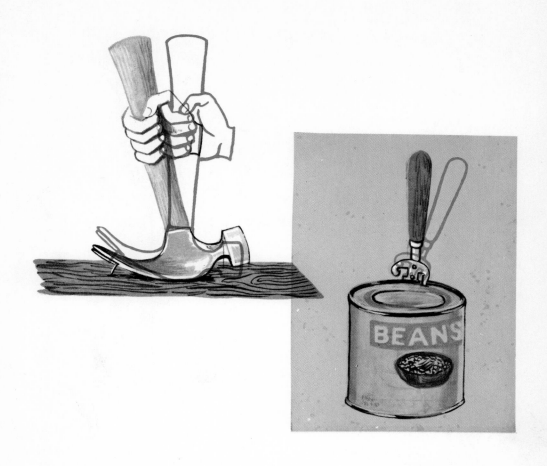

But where is the fulcrum? It is where the head of the hammer rests on the board. The fulcrum never moves.

There are many kinds of levers in your house. The old-fashioned can opener is a lever. The fulcrum is the edge of the can.

11

Double levers

Sometimes two levers are used together. Then they can do jobs that one lever can't do alone. The two levers are called a double lever. They are fastened with a screw or bolt.

A pair of scissors is a double lever. Each half is a single lever.

Try cutting a piece of paper with scissors. As your fingers come together, so do the blades.

Where is the fulcrum? The fulcrum is always the point that *doesn't move*. In scissors, the fulcrum is the screw somewhere near the middle. The handles move and the blades move. The screw doesn't move.

A pair of scissors is a double lever.

It is hard to cut something that is far from the fulcrum.

Try cutting a piece of cardboard with scissors. First, use only the tips of the blades.

The cardboard will be very hard to cut. It may not cut at all, no matter how hard you squeeze. Why? Because your fingers are *closer* to the screw than the cardboard is.

It is easy to cut something that is close to the fulcrum.

Now put the cardboard very close to the fulcrum. Your fingers are *farther* from the fulcrum than the cardboard is. You can cut it because you have more force.

Extra-heavy scissors are used to cut tin and other metals. They have short blades and very long handles. Workmen say they have *more leverage* than other scissors.

The workman's fingers are a long distance from the fulcrum. The tin sheet is very close to the fulcrum.

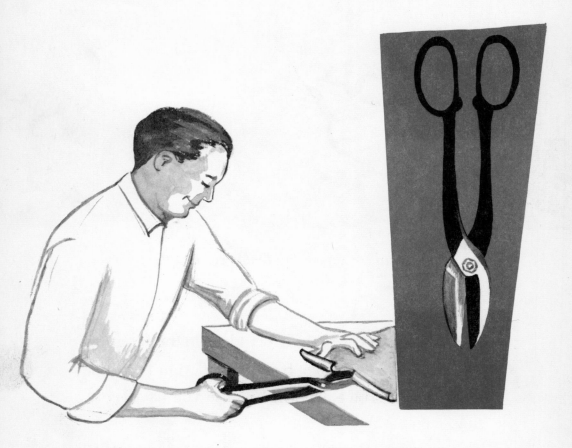

For cutting metal, scissors have long handles and short blades.

74

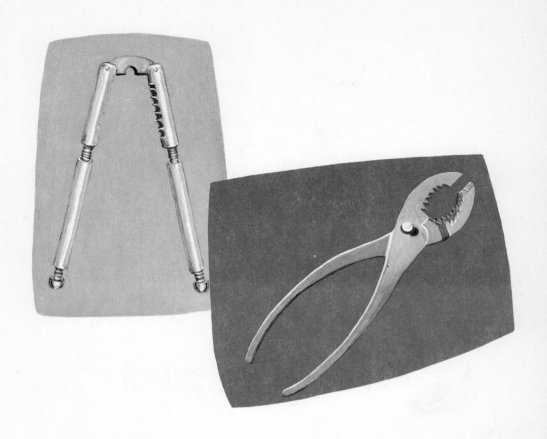

A pair of pliers is a double lever. So is a nutcracker.

A pair of pliers is also a double lever. It has short jaws that hold a nut or cut a piece of wire. The handles are long. This gives more leverage. A nutcracker is another kind of double lever.

75

12

Levers for speed

You have been looking at levers that use a little force to do a hard job. We use the long end of the lever to get more power. We can do things that would be impossible without levers. For example, you couldn't pull a nail from a board with your fingers.

But sometimes we use the short end of a lever

76

An oar is a lever that gains speed for us.

to gain speed. We have to work a little harder—but we go faster. The oar in a rowboat is a lever for speed.

You hold the oar close to the oarlock. The oarlock is the fulcrum. You are holding the short end of the lever. The long end dips into the water.

You pull back a little way at your end. The blade moves a longer distance in the water. A small movement of your hands will make a much bigger movement of the blade. You gain speed. You move much faster than if you used your own arm and hand alone as a paddle.

A fishing rod is another kind of lever for speed. You make a small movement with your hand at one end of the rod. There is a big movement at the other end.

You can see how this works with an ordinary yardstick. Hold the yardstick the way you would hold a fishing pole.

Keep the hand nearest your body still. This hand is the fulcrum. Pull up a little way with the other

A fishing rod is a lever.

hand. Notice how far and fast the other end of the yardstick moved. You have landed your fish!

Levers help us in two ways:

(1) To move heavy things with a little force.

(2) To gain speed.

13

Machines
all around you

There isn't room in this book to tell about all the machines around you. You can find many other kinds of wheels, levers, pulleys, inclined planes, wedges, and screws.

Every day you use simple machines to make work easier or to gain speed. When you walk upstairs, you are using a machine. It is an INCLINED PLANE.

When you cut food with a knife, you are using a WEDGE.

When you open one kind of jar, you may be twisting a SCREW top.

When you open another kind of jar, you may be prying the top off with a LEVER.

When you play a phonograph record, you are using a WHEEL. The record rests on the wheel and turns with it.

When you push a window up, you are using two PULLEYS. You can see them at the very top.

Keep your eyes open. When you see men digging a ditch or building a house, notice the tools they are using. How are they using these tools? You will discover some simple machines that will be fun to watch.

You can learn a lot about machines by visiting a hardware store. It has many simple machines—and some complicated ones, too.

The more you look for machines, the more of them you will see. And the more you see, the more fun you will have.

Index

STUDENT	YEAR

STUDENT	YEAR

83